A Peach Guide for Growing Homegrown Peaches

Robert F. Rangel

PAGE PUBLISHING
Conneaut Lake, PA

First originally published by Page Publishing 2024

ISBN 979-8-88960-753-3 (pbk)
ISBN 979-8-88960-760-1 (digital)

CONTENTS

INTRODUCTION

The purpose of this peach guide is to enable the peach tree grower to grow homegrown peaches efficiently and effectively. I personally planted and nurtured my peach trees by using the hands-on approach. This approach enabled me to gain empirical knowledge and experience to allow the next peach producer to build upon what I have shared and take peach growing to new heights.

Among the areas covered are the following:

1. A brief history of the peach, which includes the scientific classification, the nutritional value, and the characteristics of the peach/nectarine
2. Proper cultivating, planting, nurturing, treating, and harvesting through each stage of the entire peach production process
3. Three educational experiments offering a variety of scenarios and the resulting conclusions from each were conducted.
4. It covers four main fungi that invade peach trees and provides information for controlling fungi.

LIST OF THE MATERIALS AND SAFETY PRECAUTIONS

Materials Used to Grow Homegrown Peach Trees

- axe (large and small)
- baling wire
- calamine lotion
- first-aid kit
- full-face respirator mask
- gloves
- handheld sprayers
- hose-end sprayer (ferti-lome)
- hammer
- hat
- hoe
- insect repellant spray
- knife
- ladder
- lobbing pruning shears
- nails
- plastic containers for pesticides/materials
- pair of pliers
- pepper spray
- pocketknife
- pruner
- rake
- rope
- saw
- screwdriver
- shoes (soft sole)
- shovel
- spade
- sunscreen
- stakes (4')
- string
- towels
- water bottle
- water hose
- Weed eater
- wheelbarrow

Safety Precautions to Take When Growing Homegrown Peach Trees

1. Apply sunblock on the body part that is exposed to the sun to prevent sunburn.
2. Carry a hand pruner when checking out an orchard because there are always some twigs and small limbs that need to be pruned.
3. Always read and follow the directions of the manufacturing company on how to mix the solution with water.
4. Spray insect repellant on exposed arms, neck, and socks to repel insects before working in the orchards.
5. Take short breaks while working in the orchards to avoid heatstroke.
6. Clean and disinfect each tool after using because it might have come into contact with pests and/or diseases.
7. Check with a doctor to see if the tetanus shot is up to date.
8. Don't apply the solution on the peach trees or weeds when the wind is blowing or during the heat of the day.
9. Install a barbed wire fence around the peach orchard to keep out wild animals, such as deer that eat the tender bark of the peach trees.
10. Drink water and/or Gatorade to stay hydrated.
11. Keep your cell phone handy in case of an emergency.
12. Keep a first aid kit in case of an emergency.
13. Keep a weapon nearby in case of a varmint challenge.
14. Keep red and white Benadryl antihistamine capsules available to reduce inflammation of an insect sting.
15. Keep the Texas Poison Center Network phone number (800-222-1222) handy in case of an emergency.
16. Keep an epinephrine injector handy in case of a severe allergic reaction from a varmint bite or an insect sting.
17. Place all equipment and solutions in containers under lock and key.
18. Use common sense when working with peach trees.

19. Always wear a hat, shoes, or boots that cover feet, ankles, and part of legs to deter a varmint bite(s) or an insect sting.
20. Always wear protective gear such as a full-face gas mask, rubber gloves, a long-sleeve shirt, a wet towel placed around the neck, and a hat when spraying a solution mixture.

Purchasing Sprayers and Securing a Safe Place for the Sprayers, Pesticides, and Related Materials

Purchasing Sprayers for Spraying Pesticides

It is very important to purchase a sprayer that is efficient and effective to control the pests before they create a fatal epidemic disease that will destroy the peach trees. I chose the ferti-lome professional all-purpose hose-end sprayer because it connects to a water hose that produces water pressure to move the water to the top of the sprayer which creates a suction that siphons the liquid pesticide up the tube to the top of the sprayer head where it mixes the water with the pesticide in the head and not in the bottle. Then the pesticide mixture is forced out of the sprayer's nozzle onto the the designated spraying area. The sprayer has a brass metering dial which is mounted on top of the sprayer that selects the amount of water per gallon(s) to mix with the pesticide per ounce(s) or tablespoon(s) (two tablespoons = one ounce) according to the manufacturer's instructions to produce a certain amount of pesticide mixture to spray pests that invade the peach trees. If there is any pesticide concentrate that is left in the bottle it can be returned to the original pesticide bottle. The bottle can be washed by filling the bottle with water and turning the dial to ten to spray the pesticide residue out of the bottle quickly.

To my knowledge, this ferti-lome sprayer model is no longer being sold today, but I have seen some used ones being sold on eBay. The Tractor Supply Store sells a GroundWork 4-Pattern Hose-End Sprayer that is similar to the ferti-lome. There are several sprayers being sold on the Web that are similar to the ferti-lome.

I also purchased two ferti-lome handheld pump sprayers to wet spot spray pest manifestation areas on peach trees. Since the pesticide mixture is splashed on the manifestation pest area of a peach tree the wet pesticide stays on the area for a longer period of time than the high-pressure sprayer pesticide spray because it's pesticide evaporates faster. Thus the pump sprayer is more effective for controlling pest manifestations on peach trees. I used one pump sprayer for spraying nonorganic pesticides and the other pump sprayer to spray organic pesticides.

Purchasing Plastic Containers to Store Sprayers, Pesticides, and Related Materials

I purchased five large plastic containers to store the ferti-lome hose-end sprayers, ferti-lome handheld sprayers, pesticides, and related materials. I made sure that the sprayers, pesticide bottles, and related materials were thoroughly washed, disinfected, and dried before I placed them in the containers. All five containers were placed in the red barn under lock and key.

The following are the items that are placed in the labeled plastic containers:

- First container: I placed the ferti-lome hose-end sprayer, the ferti-lome handheld sprayer, the herbicide bottle, and related materials in the first plastic container. I labeled the plastic container FOR GRASS & WEED HERBICIDE AND RELATED MATERIALS.

- Second container: I placed the ferti-lome hose-end sprayer, the ferti-lome handheld sprayer, the insecticide bottle, and related materials in the second plastic container. I labeled the container FOR INSECT INSECTICIDE AND RELATED MATERIALS.

- Third container: I placed the ferti-lome hose-end sprayer, the ferti-lome handheld sprayer, the fungi bottle, and related materials in the third plastic container. I labeled the container FOR FUNGI FUNGICIDE AND RELATED MATERIALS.

- Fourth container: I placed the ferti-lome hose-end sprayer, the ferti-lome handheld sprayer, the organic Organocide Concentrate insecticide, fungicide, and related materials in the plastic container. I labeled the container FOR ORGANOCIDE CONCENTRATE INSECTICIDE, FUNGICIDE, AND RELATED MATERIALS.

- Fifth container: I placed the ferti-lome hose-end sprayer, the ferti-lome handheld sprayer, the neem oil concentrate container, and related materials in the fifth plastic container. I labeled the container FOR NEEM OIL CONCENTRATE AND RELATED MATERIALS.

General Information of the Peach

Sources Used to Research the Peach Trees

I began to research the peach by interviewing peach tree growers and agriculture college professors who shared their knowledge on how to grow peach trees. I then transitioned to researching information through in-depth exploration of the internet, the library, materials on how to grow peach trees from the Texas A&M AgriLife Extension Service in Rains County, and materials from the US Department of Agriculture. I became a member of the Texas Fruit Growers Association (TFGA) and attended their peach tree field trips and conferences, where I gained a wealth of information on how to grow peaches. Refer to Sources for the Texas Fruit Growers Association address.

During the time I was researching the peach, I became aware that there was a need to write a peach guide on how to grow homegrown peach trees because most of the information I obtained was in a piecemeal format geared mainly for growing large-scale commercial peach tree orchards. Thus, this guide is written by giving a step-by-step way of how I grew some homegrown peach trees.

A Brief History of the Peach

The peach's scientific name is *Prunus persica*, which means "Persian plum" due to its close relationship to the plum. The Romans and early European explorers considered the peach to be a plum because of the close similarities between the two fruits. The domesticated peach is a deciduous tree that is native to China for four thousand years. The Romans and early European explorers observed the peach tree growing in Persia, which is present-day Iran, believed it was native to Persia. The Romans and explorers were seemingly unaware the peach was brought to Persia via the Silk Road from China for two thousand years BC.

In the past, the peach was grown and consumed primarily by the wealthy throughout Asia and Europe for their personal and/or household use. Then the peach was brought to America by Spanish missionaries in 1571 to St. Simon's Island, which is located in the state of Georgia, United States. Since America remained largely an agricultural-based society through the nineteenth century, most of the peaches were homegrown mainly because of limited refrigeration.

In the twentieth century, the American economy evolved into more of an industrial society based upon the necessity of producing war materials with the onset of both World War I and World War II. When WWII ended, many Americans did not return to their farms, resulting in the disruption of practical agricultural knowledge of how to grow fruit trees.

Another reason why the knowledge of how to grow peaches among the general public was curbed was when in 1928 Thomas Midgley Jr. invented a "miracle compound" called Freon, which later General Motors and Du Pont produced Freon in 1930. Then Frigidaire produced home refrigerators using Freon and refrigerators for trucks that would transport the peaches from commercial peach farms to grocery stores throughout the United States. Therefore, the consumers could keep the peaches fresh in their own household refrigerators, which were safer to use because now it used Freon instead of the very dangerous coolants used to cool the first refrigerators produced. Therefore, more commercial farmers started growing peaches to sell peaches commercially because it was a peach bonanza to sell.

However, today there is a movement to plant your own homegrown food, especially among Americans, who have the burning desire to work with Mother Nature's earth by getting their hands soiled and obtaining the gratification of growing their own peach trees. Unfortunately, some Americans don't have the knowledge of how to grow homegrown peach trees; therefore, many of the peach trees that are planted expire soon after being planted.

Consequently, the desire to plant and grow another batch of peach trees quickly diminishes. Thus, in order to keep the peach trees from expiring, the peach guide was written to provide some knowledge on how I grew peach trees that didn't expire after I planted them.

The Scientific Classification of the Peach

Kingdom: Plantae
Order: Rosales
Subgenus: Prunus
Family: Rosaceae
Species: P. persica
Genus: Prunus
Scientific Name: *Prunus persica*

The Nutritional Value of the Peach

The nutritional value of the edible parts of the peach per 100 grams, with percentages relative to the United States and the source being the USDA Nutrient database, are as follows:

Energy: 40 Kcal
Dietary fibers: 1.5 g
Sugars: 8.4 g

Carbohydrates: 9.5 g
Fats: 0.3 g
Proteins: 0.9 g
Vitamins: 6.6 mg

The peach is rich in vitamin A and has vital minerals such as potassium, fluoride, and iron.

Characteristics of the Peach

The peach has glossy-green elliptic lanceolate-shaped leaves, generally 7–15 cm broad. The peach blossom is light pink to light purple in color, with no more than five petals that bloom before the leaves in the spring. The blossom is called the "pink lady," which symbolizes immortality, while the peach tree symbolizes longevity. The peach fruit is developed from a single ovary that has two ovules. One of the ovules ripens into a fleshy exterior that becomes the edible part of the peach. The other ovule is fertilized and develops into a seed that is encased in the shell of hardwood called a stone that is located in the center of the peach. This is the reason why peaches are called stone fruits.

The peach is composed of three main layers, which are the exocarp, mesocarp, and endocarp. The exocarp is the outer layer that also includes the skin of the peach; the mesocarp is the fleshy edible part of the peach that surrounds the endocarp. The endocarp hardens to a stone and adheres closely to the seed within. Refer to figure 1 for a cross-section drawing of the peach.

The flesh of the peach can be either white or yellow, with both having some blush on the skin. The white-flesh peach has a sweet taste while the yellow peach has a tangy taste due to the presence of an acid. As a general rule, Asians prefer the sweet white-flesh peach while Americans and Europeans prefer the acidic yellow flesh. A good example of a sweet white flesh peach is the Belle of Georgia peach that originated in 1870 in the state of Georgia.

Characteristics of the Nectarine

A peach is considered to be a peach because the skin has a fuzz to protect it against insects. If the peach skin doesn't have fuzz, it is called a nectarine, but by the same token, it is still considered a peach without fuzz. Basically, the first nectarine was a genetic mutation of a peach. Genetic studies claim that the nectarine was produced because it lacks the gene that makes the peach fuzzy. The peach flesh can be white or yellow with a red blush, but the nectarine's flesh can only be yellow with a red blush skin because it doesn't produce non-acid white flesh.

Three Types of Peaches

The peach is considered to be a drupe because it has a single large wood-encased seed called a stone. The peach is divided into three main types due to its stone types. These types are as follows:

1.   Freestone: The peach stone does not cling to its flesh.
2.   Semi-freestone: The peach stone partially clings to its flesh.
3.   Clingstone: The peach stone clings to its flesh.

The difference between the freestone and the clingstone is that the freestone peach flesh can be removed from the pit easily. The freestone is generally good for eating by hand, cooking, baking, and canning. In contrast, the clingstone peach flesh is attached to the pit, and it is more difficult to remove from the pit. It is generally ideal for eating but not desirable for cooking, baking, or canning since they are difficult to prep. The clingstone is typically smaller than the freestone, but it is sweeter, which makes it perfect to make jellies.

Chilling Hours of the Peach

Before the peach trees can properly produce peaches, the peach trees need to obtain their required amount of chilling hours during the dormant stage, which starts in late fall to early spring. The chilling hours cause the peach tree to go through hormonal changes for flowering_and fruit production. The chilling-hour temperatures range from 32 to 45 degrees Fahrenheit for the peach tree.

Different varieties of the peach tree require different amounts of chilling hours, and chilling hours directly affect the corresponding harvest-time window. As a general rule, if peach varieties have fewer chilling-hour requirements, then the peach trees will generally produce peaches earlier during the harvest period. The Earligrande, Early Amber, and Rio Grande varieties require 450 chilling hours or less, and they ripen in May instead of June, July, and August. I would not plant these peach varieties in Northeast Texas because it freezes throughout spring, and since these varieties bloom in spring, a freeze would destroy their blossoms; thus, no delicious peaches would be produced.

I chose the Loring peach tree to grow and experiment because the Loring is a freestone, which requires 750 chilling hours in order to flower and fruit properly. The 750-chilling-hour requirement is the right amount of hours because the peach experiment sites are located in Northeast Texas, where it is colder for a longer period than in other parts of Texas. Therefore, the Loring receives the sufficient amount of cold weather to obtain the 750 chilling hours it needs.

Dormant Stages of the Peach

1. The dormant stage is called the rest stage. This is the stage when the required chilling hours are being accumulated. During the chilling period, key chemical reactions will occur so that the peach trees can flower and fruit properly.
2. The quiescence stage is when the peach trees have obtained the chilling-hour requirement. The trees are in an inactive phase until warm weather occurs and the buds break and grow.

Budding and Grafting Peach Trees to Make Them Cultivars and Nematode Resistant

Budding and Grafting Peach Trees to Breed Them into Cultivars

There are approximately two thousand varieties of peach trees in the world, and three hundred are grown in the United States. Most of these varieties are considered to be cultivars because they were scientifically developed by horticulturists by using selective breeding methods such as budding and grafting to produce the cultivars. Since these peach trees, such as the Loring, are bred into cultivars, it will not be true to seed, but the peach trees grown from seed will be true to seed.

Nurseries Grafting Peach Trees to Nemaguard Root Stock to Make the Peach Trees Root-Knot Nematode Resistant

Nematodes are microscopic wormlike parasites that feed on peach trees' root hairs that damage peach tree roots, especially if the trees are not nematode protected. In order to control the nematodes, the peach tree commercial nurseries graft the peach trees to the Nemaguard rootstocks in order for the peach trees to become nematode resistant. Then knots form when the Nemaguard rootstocks are grafted to the peach trees.

The nurseries will sell the peach trees as nematode-resistant peach trees. However, the peach trees that are Nemaguard nematode resistant are only protected against the root knot nematodes but not against the ring nematodes. If the peach trees are attacked by the ring nematodes, the county extension agent should provide some material to select a nematocide that will control the ring nematodes.

Since the Loring peach trees were grafted to Nemaguard rootstocks, the peach trees are resistant only to the root knot nematodes. In the event some of the peach trees had acquired some ring Nematodes in sites A and/or B, I would have immediately applied nematocide that was suggested by the county extension agent material on the peach trees' roots to control the ring nematodes.

Nematodes can cause bacterial cankers on the peach trees, causing the peach trees to expire. If the peach tree(s) expire due to nematodes, the infected peach tree(s) should be eradicated and burned in the burn pile or barrel. Then I would spray the planting hole with the nematocide and cover the hole with some soil from the sandy loam pile.

The Nemaguard rootstocks not only protect peach trees against root knot nematodes but also help the peach trees grow vigorously and helps the trees to be freeze and disease resistant. Thus, many of the peach tree varieties commercially sold today are grafted to the Nemaguard rootstocks. The Nemared, Lovell, Halford, and Guardian are other rootstocks that are used for nematode-resistant protection.

Planting Zones of the Peach Trees

The peach trees generally grow better in zones 4 to 8 in the United States, with zone 6 being the best growing zone due to its mild climate in addition to having enough chilling hours to grow several varieties of peach trees. I planted the Loring peach trees in Rains County, which is located in Northeast Texas.

I obtained the Rains County planting zone by using Google. I typed the address zip code of the peach trees' planting sites, plus the words *planting zone* on Google's screen. Then Google indicated that the property planting zone for this address in Rains County was 8a hardiness planting zone, which was a cold zone, which lasted longer throughout winter and spring. Since the Loring required 750 chilling hours, this 8a hardiness planting zone was all right for planting the Loring peach trees.

Planting Six Different Varieties of Peach Trees

Planting Six Different Varieties of Peach Trees in Order to Have Peaches throughout Harvesttime

The following are six different peach tree varieties that could be planted in the 8a hardiness planting zone in order to have peaches throughout the harvest months, which are June, July, and August:

1. Sentinel: Semi-freestone 850 CH, large yellow, ripe: early June
2. Loring: freestone 750 CH, large yellow, ripe: late June
3. Elberta: freestone 850 CH, large yellow, ripe: mid July
4. Red skin: freestone 750 CH, red skin, ripe: mid July
5. Red globe: freestone 850 CH, red skin, ripe: late July
6. Frank: clingstone 750 CH, large yellow, ripe: early August

Obtaining a State of Texas Pesticide License and Notifying the State of Texas Private Pesticide Applicator License and Utility Locator Service

Texas Department of Agriculture Private Pesticide Applicator License

Since the private pesticide applicator license is the function of the Texas Department of Agriculture, it is best for the person who is interested in obtaining a pesticide applicator license to contact the Texas Department of Agriculture to find out how to obtain a private pesticide applicator license. Refer to Sources to obtain the Texas Department of Agriculture–Pesticide License address.

Texas Utility Locater Service When Planting One or More Trees

Texas law requires a landowner acting as his own contractor to notify the Utility Locator Service whenever he or she plans to plant a tree or trees. The landowner needs to call the statewide number 811 or submit an online request through www.texas811.org. to obtain information before planting a tree or trees.

Selecting Two Planting Sites, Dividing Sites into Small Orchards to Plant Peach Trees, and Cultivating a Site That Was Not Conducive for Growing Peach Trees

Selecting Two Planting Sites to Plant and Grow Peach Trees

Two planting sites were selected that had the appropriate soil to grow peach trees; this is sandy loam, which is abundant in Northeast Texas. The sites also had access to well and city water, and it had a good elevation for water drainage.

Proper water drainage is vital for peach trees because they "don't like wet feet." If the peach tree roots stay submerged in water for a short period of time, the roots could obtain root rot. Another way the peach tree roots may obtain root rot such as Armillaria is when the peach trees are planted close to oak trees. The reason is that oak trees tend to acquire Armillaria fungus, and this fungus could invade the peach tree roots. If the Armillaria fungus invades the peach tree roots, it's difficult to keep the peach tree from expiring.

The Two Peach Tree Sites Were Divided into Three Small Peach Tree Orchards per Site, and Each Small Orchard Was Labeled to Conduct an Experiment

The first planting site was labeled as site, A and it was divided into three equal small peach tree orchards where I planted and grew the peach trees to conduct three experiments. The first orchard was labeled controlled orchard 1 (CO 1), the second orchard controlled orchard 2 (CO 2), and the third orchard controlled orchard 3 (CO 3).

The other site that was at another nearby location, the site was labeled as site B, and it was also divided into three equal small peach tree orchards. The first orchard was labeled as the independent variable orchard 1 (IVO 1), the second orchard as independent variable orchard 2 (IVO 2), and the third orchard as the independent variable orchard 3 (IVO 3).

After I planted the different types and sizes of peach trees at sites A and B, I conducted education experiments 1, 2, and 3 by comparing the CO 1 peach trees with the IVO 1 trees, the CO 2 peach trees with the IVO 2 trees, and the CO 3 peach trees with the IVO 3 trees to determine if any of the independent variable orchard peach trees produced healthier peaches than the control orchard trees.

A Peach Tree Site That Was Not Conducive for Growing Peaches and the Site Soil Was Cultivated to Grow Peaches

A good example of a site that was not conducive for growing peaches but was cultivated to grow peach trees was written in the *The Dallas Morning News* on September 26, 1899, Sunday edition on page 16, in a compiled-stories-and-pictures features highlighting Texas history. This story, "The 20th Century Through The Eyes of Texas," tells how a French Texan by the name of Gustave Santerre, who lived on a limestone bluff overlooking Dallas in the 1900, cultivated the bluff to plant peach trees by hacking off mountain cedar and chiseling holes with a pick and/or blasting the holes with dynamite.

After Gustave made the holes, he filled the holes with the appropriate soil, minerals, and nutrients to grow peach trees. Gustave then planted the peach trees in the holes, and the peach trees grew well and produced delicious healthy peaches as the peaches produced by peach trees that were planted in the Dallas area.

Selecting Fertile Soil and Testing the
Soil for Growing Peach Trees

Selecting Soil for Planting and Growing Peach Trees

Peach trees grow best in soil types such as coarse-textured sand, gravelly loam, and sandy loam. Peach trees do not grow well in heavy-clay or fine-textured soil. These two types of soils have the undesirable tendency to become waterlogged and/or have poor drainage; thus, peach trees will not grow well in this type of soil.

Also, peach trees don't grow well in desert arid regions because the soil has saline soil in the subsurface layer. The presence of saline will curb peach tree rooting, keeping the tree from obtaining minerals, nutrients, and water. The saline will cause the peach tree to have abnormal defoliation and leaf scorching. Therefore, it is very important not to plant peach trees in the desert, but there is a peach tree by the name of Desert Gold that will grow in the desert, providing it is watered.

Testing Peach Tree Orchards' Soil for Minerals and pH

I tested the soil for the two peach tree sites by obtaining several random soil samples of sites A and B orchards and sending the samples to the Texas Agriculture Extension Service Soil, Water, and Forage Testing Lab, where the soil was analyzed to find out if the soil had some mineral deficiencies. The testing lab also gave the pH of the soil to find out if the soil was acidic or alkaline.

I obtained the pre-addressed soil testing bags from the Rains County AgriLife Extension Service agent and sent the random samples of the planting sites A and B to the Texas AgriLife Extension Service Soil, Water, and Forage Testing Lab to test the soils. When I received the Texas AgriLife Extension Service (TAES) soil test results, it indicated that the soil was slightly deficient in phosphorus and potassium; therefore, in order to correct this deficiency, I added Southern Ag All-Purpose Granular Fertilizer (10 10 10)—Balanced

Plant Nutrients to the A and B planting sites. The reason why I used this fertilizer was because it contains nitrogen, phosphorus, and potassium, which are essential for good plant growth and root development.

In addition, the fertilizer includes boron, iron, magnesium, manganese, zinc, and plant nutrients. A mineral is a naturally occurring inorganic element that has a crystal structure that is made of a definite atomic arrangement, and a nutrient is a substance that provides nourishment that is essential to maintain life such as proteins and vitamins.

As per the pH of the soil, it was acidic with a 6.6 pH +/- throughout the A and B planting sites. Although the pH 6.6 pH + was conducive to grow peaches because peaches can grow well between pH 6.6 pH and 6.9 pH, I prefer to grow peaches at 6.8 pH or 6.9 pH. Therefore, I applied agriculture lime on the A and B sites until the soil pH readings were 6.8 pH or 6.9 pH. If the soil had been alkaline with a reading of 7.1 pH +, I would have added some sulfur to make the peach soil slightly acid with a reading of 6.8 pH or 6.9 pH.

Purchasing a Soil Test Kit and a Test Apparatus to Test the Soil Moisture and Its pH

Purchasing a Soil Test Kit

Since I needed to test the soil of the peach orchards often, I purchased a soil test kit from the Web. The soil test kit that I purchased tested for the essential minerals such as nitrogen, phosphorus, and potassium, which are the main elements that peach trees need to grow roots, limbs, leaves, and peaches. Therefore, after I planted the peach trees, I frequently tested the soil especially around the peach trees to check if the soil had been depleted of minerals and nutrients that were absorbed by the root system of the peach trees to make the peach trees grow and produce healthy peaches.

In the event the soil test showed that the soil was lacking minerals and/or nutrients, I immediately fertilized the soil and watered it so that the fertilizer would soak into the soil; therefore, the peach tree root system could efficiently absorb the minerals and nutrients so that the peach trees could grow and produce healthy peaches.

Purchasing Soil Moisture and pH Kits

As per the moisture and pH test kit, the soil test apparatus had two metal rods to stick into the soil to test for moisture and the pH of the soil. If I was testing for moisture, I would stick the testing apparatus' two metal rods into the soil and turn the dial to moisture. If the dial showed that the soil lacked moisture, I would water the area soil immediately.

Water is considered to be a nutrient, so the peach trees need water to grow as it is well known. Then when I checked the soil for pH, I turned the dial to pH, and if it gave a pH reading of 7 pH +, it would be too alkaline to grow peaches because the peach trees grow best when the soil is slightly acidic, such as 6.9 pH. Therefore, I would apply sulfur until the soil had a reading of a 6.9 pH or 6.8. If the pH dial showed a pH 6.5 pH or less, the soil would be too acidic to grow peaches; therefore, I would apply agriculture lime around the peach trees' trunks until it had a pH reading of 6.8 pH to 6.9 pH, because peach trees grow in a slightly acidic soil.

As a general rule, the peach trees that grow in an excessive alkaline soil have leaves that tend to lose their color and stunt the growth of the peach trees. If the soil is too acidic, it will cause the leaves to wilt and drop. Therefore, it is very important to keep the pH levels of the soil between 6.8 pH and 6.9 pH for growing peach trees. Since the planting peach sites A and B were close to some pine trees, the soil of the peach trees' pH were usually too acidic because the pine tree needles are acidic. Consequently, I had to apply agriculture lime on the peach tree soil several times to make the soil slightly acidic with a pH of 6.8 to 6.9.

Purchasing Peach Trees

Purchasing Tall and Short Bare-Root Peach Trees

The Texas Pecan Nursery, Inc. provided me with a brochure illustrating the different varieties of peaches and other fruit trees that were for sale with a price list via the internet. I made sure I ordered the peach trees on July 1 because this is the date the peach trees go on sale and the trees sell fast. The peach trees were ready to pick up in November. I purchased some wholesale bare-root peach trees because as a general rule the bare-root peach trees cost less than peach trees that are sold in burlap sacks or in gallon container. In addition, the bare-root peach trees have more roots that are thicker and longer than peach trees that are not bare-root.

I picked up my peach trees at the Texas Pecan Nursery, Inc. in the month of November, and I temporarily heeled in the peach trees in the sandy loam pile until I got ready to plant them during the dormant stage of winter. According to the *Old Farmer's Almanac Garden Plants*, winter starts on December 21, which is the first day of the winter solstice, and it is the shortest day and the longest night of the year.

If an individual wants to obtain information about purchasing some of these peach trees, refer to Sources in this peach guide to obtain the Texas Pecan Nursery, Inc. address and phone number.

Cultivating the Peach Orchards and Calculating the Number of Peach Trees to Plant

Cultivating the Orchards to Plant Peach Trees in Winter

I sprayed the orchard's site surfaces in early June for herbaceous weeds, fungi, and insects. Next, I dug the planting holes in November where each tree was to be planted right after December 21, which is the start of the winter solstice. I took out all the dead weeds from sites A and B, but I left the grass between the peach tree rows to create a grass mat so that small vehicles would not get stuck in the mud when it rained.

I dug square holes instead of round holes to plant the peach trees because square holes were wider to spread the root system of the bare-root peach trees in the planting hole. The square holes were 3 feet by 3 feet wide and approximately 3 feet deep, depending on the length of the tree roots, because peach tree roots are about 3 feet long unless minerals, nutrients, and water are not readily available.

Care should be given to ensure the planting square holes are not deeper than the length of the root system because the roots will continue to sink into the planting hole until they reach the bottom of the hole after they are planted. If this happens, the nematode graft knot, which is located at the base of the tree trunk, might sink below the ground, and this might keep the peach trees from growing properly. In fact, some peach tree growers believe that peach trees will grow better if some of their roots are exposed to sunlight. This is called root flash exposure.

I then dug the planting holes for the peach trees in the A and B sites orchards. The holes were dug in rows whereby the distances were 15 feet apart from each other. Then the peach tree rows distance were 15 feet apart. By planting 15 feet apart on the rows and the rows being 15 feet apart, the peach trees shouldn't have to compete for water, minerals, and nutrients.

In addition, some peach tree growers claim that peach trees grow faster, healthier, and produce more peaches by trimming some of the treetops when the trees are planted. The peach trees should also be planted and covered with the same soil in the square holes that were dug. I also wrapped chicken wire around the tender trunks of the newly planted peach trees to protect them against varmints, and I made sure the chicken wire was not wrapped too tight around the tree trunks to prevent girdling.

How to Calculate the Number of Peach Trees to Plant per Acre

Some peach tree growers plant trees according to this formula used to determine how many trees they want to plant per acre. For example, if the distance between the trees in a row is 15 feet, then multiply it by 15 feet, which is the distance between the peach tree rows, and it equals a woodlot area of 225 square feet. Then divide 43,560 square feet in an acre by 225 square feet woodlot; it will equal 194 peach trees that can be planted in the acre.

If a peach tree farmer wants to plant a large number of peach trees per acre, then planting 194 peach trees could be a good number of peach trees to plant in an acre. Although the peach tree farmer must keep in mind that the more peach trees planted per acre, the more minerals, nutrients, and water the peach trees will need to grow healthy to produce delicious peaches.

Pesticides to Spray the A and B Planting Site Surfaces before Planting the Peach Trees and Some Information about Pests

Spraying Nonorganic and Organic Pesticides on the A and B Site Surfaces

In order to obtain the nonorganic pesticides such as herbicides, insecticides, and fungicides to spray the planting sites A and B land surface to control pests, the county extension agent provided a nonorganic list of these pesticides. Therefore, a herbicide was selected from the list to control herbaceous plants and weeds. This nonorganic herbicide was sprayed on the A and B surfaces at the beginning of the month of June with a ferti-lome hose-end sprayer, except for the small orchard IVO 3 located in site B. Then in mid-June, the nonorganic insecticide and fungicide were selected from the list and applied on the site A and B surfaces, except for the IVO 3 surface in site B. The nonorganic pesticides are nonselective, which means it can harm annual and perennial plants.

As per site B, the small orchard IVO 3 surface was sprayed with an organic herbicide that controlled herbaceous plants and weeds at the beginning of June. The IVO 3 ground surface was sprayed with Concentrate organic Eco Garden Pro-Organic Vinegar Weed and Grass Killer by Eco Living Solutions. This herbicide can be purchased on the Web. Although the herbicide is organic, it is still considered to be nonselective, which mean it could still harm annuals and perennials but not as severe as a nonorganic herbicide. The organic herbicide is biodegradable and safe for groundwater. After the herbicide is applied and dries, it is safe for pets, kids, fish, and livestock. The organic herbicide was sprayed with a ferti-lome hose-end sprayer.

Then in mid-June, the site B IVO 3 surface was sprayed with Captain Jack's Neem Max Concentrate to control insects, bugs, and fungi. The neem oil is also a dormant spray that can be used for every season. The Captain Jack's Neem Max Concentrate can be purchased over the counter at farm supply stores, Home Depot, Lowes, and the Web. A ferti-lome hose-end sprayer was used to spray the organic neem oil on the IVO 3 of the site B surface to control pests and the soil returns to normal in six months to plant.

Some Information about Pests

The term *pest* refers to herbaceous plants, weeds, insects, bugs, fungi, mites, and varmints. As per insects, not all insects are destructive in nature because there are some insects that are beneficial insects, such as the miniature trichogramma wasps that get rid of cabbageworms, tomato hornworms, codling months, cutworms, armyworms, webworms, corn borers, cane borers, and fruitworms. If a plant or tree grower decides to use the trichogramma wasps, then he or she shouldn't use a pesticide on the plants or trees because the pesticide might injure the trichogramma wasps unless the pesticide is trichogramma wasp friendly.

Also, if the trichogramma wasps are used, then a small plate full of water should be placed beside the wasps when they arrive because they are very thirsty after being on the long trip to get to their destination. These wasps can be purchased on the Web.

The honeybee is a beneficial insect because it pollinates the blossoms of plants and trees in order for fertilization to occur, thus producing fruit and seed. In contrast, the mosquito is a vector because it transmits a pathogen, disease, or parasite from one animal or plant to another. As per bugs, they are a particular type of insect that have mouthparts that are modified for piercing and sucking juice out of fruits.

Pesticides to Spray Peach Trees at A and B Site Orchards and Information on the Nonorganic and Organic Pesticides to Spray Pests

Selecting Nonorganic Pesticides for Spraying Peach Trees at A and B Sites Small Orchards

After the winter solstice, which is on December 21, the peach trees were planted at sites A and B, and later in spring, the trees were sprayed with a nonorganic insecticide and a fungicide that had copper because copper controls fungi very well. The county extension agent provided a list of nonorganic insecticides and fungicide to spray the peach trees. A ferti-lome hose-end sprayer was used to spray the peach trees with the county agent nonorganic pesticides.

Selecting the Organic Pesticide to Spray the IVO 3 on Site B

Organic Organicide 3-in-1 Concentrate was selected to spray the peach trees planted at the IVO 3 during the spring and summer months for insects, fungi, and mites, while the Captain Jack's Neem Max Concentrate was selected to spray fungi, insects, and mites in August, fall or winter.

The reason the IVO 3 peach trees were sprayed with organic pesticides was because these trees were being compared with the

CO 3 peach trees, which were sprayed with nonorganic pesticides to determine if the nonorganic pesticides were more effective than the organic pesticides to control insects, fungi, and mites. The results for this experiment are given in the subsequent Education Experiment 3 of this peach guide.

Providing Information for the Organic Organocide Spray Concentrate

Organocide is a honeybee-beneficial insect-friendly organic pesticide. Therefore, the honeybee becomes a pollinator by pollinating reproductive parts in the peach blossom. The honeybee transfers the pollen from the male anther to the female stigma, which will fertilize the peach flower that will later yield fruit and seed.

Another reason why Organocide was used was because it controls small insects such as mites that are constantly trying to enter the peach blossoms before and after the blossoms open. If these small insects enter the blossoms, they will disrupt the pollination and fertilization process inside the blossoms. If this happens, the peaches could become abnormal and/or expire. Therefore, the spring green-tip buds were sprayed before the blossoms opened in order to control the small insects before they damaged the green buds of the blossoms.

After the blossoms opened, I continued to spray the peach trees according to a spraying program 2 with Organocide, but I never sprayed inside of the peach blossoms because it would disrupt the pollination and fertilization processes. If this type of disruption occurs, the peach trees will not produce peaches.

Organocide is an organic pesticide that is mild but effective because it is made up of a specific blend of potassium sorbate, sesame oil, lecithin, and edible fish oil. Therefore, since Organocide is organic, the peaches should continue to have their original peach perfume aroma and peachy keen taste that individuals love to smell and taste when they eat the peach.

Although peach trees were sprayed with organic Organocide and neem oil, the peach trees are not considered to be organic peach trees. In order for peach trees to be certified as organic peach trees, the United States Department of Agriculture (USDA) must be the one to certify the peach trees as organic peaches. The peach tree grower who wants to certify his or her peach trees as organic must contact the United States Department of Agriculture (USDA) to learn how to certify the peach trees as organic. The USDA phone number is 202-720-3252.

Reason for Not Spraying Nonorganic and Organic Bactericide on Peach Trees Unless There Is a Bacteria Manifestation on the Peach Trees

The reason why I didn't spray the sites A and B peach tree orchards with a nonorganic or organic bactericide was because bacteria plays a major role for producing nutritional soil for the peach trees. Although if I had observed signs of bacteria on the peach trees such as a canker and/or the peach leaves being infected, with reddish-purple spots that often have a white center, I would have summoned the county extension agent so he could determine if the peach trees did indeed acquire a bacteria. If the county extension agent determined that bacteria did exist on sites A and B but not on IV0 3, I would use one of the nonorganic solutions that control bacteria on the county extension agent's lists to spray on the manifestation of bacteria.

I used a handheld ferti-lome pump sprayer in order to wet-spray the bacteria manifestation on the peach tree. If I had used a ferti-lome hose-end sprayer, the spraying would be so excessive that there might be an overabundance of bactericide that would drip on the ground that might harm some of the bacteria that are preparing nutritional soil for the peach trees.

If the bacteria manifestation was located in the site B IVO 3, I would use Neem Max because it is cold-pressed, which means none of the ingredients have been extracted; thus, it controls bacteria. I would use a handheld ferti-lome sprayer to wet-spray the neem oil on the bacteria manifestation, and there wouldn't be an overabundance of bactericide dripping on the ground that would harm the soil bacteria that is preparing nutritional soil for the peach trees.

Neem Max is a good organic insecticide, fungicide, and bactericide. Therefore, the site B IVO 3 peach trees were sprayed with neem oil before fall because it controls pests such as codling moths and meal worms. It also prevents black spots, rust leaves spot, leaf spot, and scab disease. One of the main devastating pests that neem oil concentrate controls are bores. Therefore, neem oil mixture was sprayed on the site B IVO 3 in early August before the autumnal equinox, which is before the September 22 autumnal equinox, because during this time the female bores descend on the peach trunks. Then the female bores will lay their eggs in the trunk cracks, and the eggs will hatch within 10 days. Next the larvae will burrow into the tree trunks' xylem and phloem, creating a blockage of water and nutrient flow throughout the peach trees, causing them to expire.

Precautions Taken when Spraying Pesticides

Precautions Taken When Spraying Pesticides on the A and B Planting Site Surfaces and Peach Trees

I always read and follow the instructions of a manufacturer's products on how to mix and apply their pesticide concentrates with water to create the pesticide mixtures to control herbaceous plants, weeds, bacteria, fungi, insects, and diseases. I used the ferti-lome hose-end sprayer because it automatically mixes the pesticide with the water according to the manufacturer's instructions to produce the pesticide mixture.

I always wear a full-face gas mask to protect me from dangerous moistures and gases. I also wear a long-sleeve shirt, a hat, gloves, and a big red handkerchief wrapped around my neck so that the pesticide mixture could not invade my body. I keep a bottle of calamine lotion in the first aid case in the event I have an allergic reaction to a poisonous plant, such as poison ivy. Since I took these precautions, I didn't have an insect to sting or a poisonous plant to invade my body's skin or have any reaction to the pesticide mixtures I sprayed.

After I completed spraying the two planting site surfaces with nonorganic and organic pesticides, I kept humans and/or pets away from the sprayed sites for a few days because some humans and/or pets might be allergic to the non-organic pesticides that were sprayed. I washed and disinfected the equipment I used to spray the peach tree orchards. I then placed the sprayers, equipment, and materials in the appropriate plastic container after every spraying. I also washed my clothes and cleaned my boots that I was wearing because they might be contaminated with the mixture that I had sprayed. I followed all these precautions because as the adage states, an ounce of prevention is worth a pound of cure.

Testing the Water and Watering Peach Trees

Testing City and Well Water for Bacteria, Fungi, Minerals, Nutrients, and pH

When I selected the peach orchard sites, I made sure the sites had plenty of water available. The location I chose for the sites were in Rains County, which is in Northeast Texas. The peach orchard sites had access to both city and well water. Since city and well water need to be tested often for pests and diseases, I therefore purchased test kits to test for coliform bacteria, fungi, and chlorine. I also purchased a pH kit to test the city and well water because if the water is too acidic or alkaline it can be harmful to the peach trees. There are several water and pH tests kits that are sold through the Web and farm supply stores.

The city drinking water was tested for bacteria, lead, pesticides, nitrates, nitrites, chlorine, and hardness by using water test kits. The city drinking water tested negative for all these items except for some chlorine, which was harmless. Next, the pH of the city water was tested by using a water pH test kit, and the drinking water had a 7 pH, which is considered to be pure water. The city water was used to water the peach trees in Site B IVO 1, IVO 2, IVO 3 by using a drip irrigation system.

The well water was tested for coliform bacteria, fungi, parasites, nitrates and nitrites, hardness, and the pH by using a well-water pH test kit. The results of all these items were negative, including water hardness, which is considered to be the amount of dissolved calcium and magnesium in the water. There is also an easy home test for coliform bacteria. The instructions state to fill a jar with well water and wait for forty-eight hours. If the water in the jar turns yellow, then the water tests positive for coliform bacteria.

When I tested the well water for pH, it had a reading of 6.9, which was slightly acidic in which the peach trees grow well. I used well water for Site A CO 1, CO 2, and CO 3 peach trees.

Watering Peach Trees When Water Is Not Available

In the event the city and the well water were not available, I conducted a way to water the peach trees at the A and B sites. I purchased a plastic thirty-gallon container, which had a battery-operated motor connected to it and had a sprayer attached to it. This type of sprayer is used to spray pesticides on peach trees, and I brought the sprayer at a farmer's supply store.

When I sprayed the peach trees with water, I placed the sprayer on top of a flatbed pull wagon. I easily pulled the wagon between the peach tree rows, which were fifteen feet apart, and sprayed the peach trees. I concluded that spraying with this type of sprayer was effective for watering the peach trees.

After watering the peach trees, I became aware that it was very important never to use the thirty-gallon plastic container to spray nonorganic and organic pesticide. The reason for not using the thirty-gallon container is because if the container is used to spray pesticides it might have some pesticide residue left in container after it is washed. If the container is used to water the peach trees and the container has residue, it might affect the peach trees in a negative health manner.

Therefore, I wrote on the thirty-gallon plastic container in large letters, THIS CONTAINER IS ONLY USED FOR WATERING THE PEACH TREES AND IT IS NOT TO BE USED TO SPRAY NON-ORGANIC AND ORGANIC PESTICIDE.

Some of techniques that I used to conserve water was to plant the peach tree on the rows that are fifteen feet apart, and the peach trees rows were fifteen feet apart so that the peach trees will not have to compete for water, minerals, and nutrients. I watered the peach trees in the morning to allow the trees to absorb the water during the heat of the day and so that the tree trunks will be dry in the evening to control fungi growth because fungi favor high moisture and moderate temperatures to grow fast.

Furthermore, I pruned the peach trees lightly to reduce transpiration, which is loss of water vapor through the stomata of the peach trees. These stomata are located on the peach tree leaves and stems. The peach trees lose a lot of their water through transpiration. Light pruning also encourages healthy growth of peach trees and removes dying limbs that waste the tree's resources.

Purchasing a Drip Irrigation Watering System

I purchased the drip irrigation water system from the Irrigation-Mart Company because this company provided an irrigation kit that had all the necessary materials such as accessories, fittings, pressure valve, time clock, and tubing to install the drip irrigation watering system in the IVO 1, IVO 2, and IVO 3. I sent the Irrigation-Mart Company a grid by giving the dimensions for the IVO 3 orchards. The Irrigation-Mart Company sent me a do-it-yourself (DIY) kit to install the drip irrigation watering system in the IVO 1, IVO 2, and IVO 3 peach orchards.

After installing the watering system, I could water the 3 IVO at the same time or separately. I could water the peach trees from one hour to six hours by setting the clock on how many hours I wanted to water. Also, by watering with a drip watering system, the water will seep deep into the soil; thus, the peach tree roots will grow thicker and longer by growing deep into the soil to obtain moisture. Refer to Sources to obtain the address of Irrigation-Mart Co.

Education Experiment 1

Criteria Used to Evaluate the Water Experiment 1

This experiment was conducted to find out if watering the bare-root six-feet-tall trees in IVO 1 that were watered with city water by using a drip irrigation watering system produced more peaches than watering the bare-root six-feet-tall trees in the CO 1 by using well water. The IVO 1 and CO 1 peach trees received the same kind and amount of fertilizer throughout the experiment.

Well water: The six-feet-tall bare-root peach trees in CO 1 were watered with well water whenever the soil test indicated that the soil lacked moisture. The peach trees were watered with a water hose and water sprinklers until the moist test indicated that the soil was moist, meaning it had sufficient water.

City water: The six-feet-tall bare-root peach trees in the IVO 1 were watered with city water by using a drip irrigation system. The IVO 1 peach trees were watered immediately when the soil test indicated that the soil lacked moisture. The drip irrigation system has a pressure valve apparatus that has a time clock that can be set to water the IVO 1 peach trees up to six hours at a time.

The peach tree variety used: Loring peach trees

Experiment duration: Two-and-a-half years

The number and height of Lorings used to conduct experiment 1 for CO1: There were ten six-feet one-inch thick bare-root Loring trees to conduct experiment 1 for CO 1.

The number and height of Lorings used to conduct experiment 1 for IVO 1: There were ten six-feet one-inch thick bare-root Loring trees to conduct experiment 1 for IVO 1.

Fertilizer: Both the CO 1 peach tree and the IVO 1 were fertilized with the same fertilizer, which was the Southern Ag All-Purpose

(10 10 10) that was administered at the same amount and time during the two-and-a-half-years experiment duration.

First evaluation: The first evaluation was conducted in the month of June during harvest time, which was six months from the time the CO 1 peach trees and the IVO 1 peach trees were planted after December 21. The CO 1 peach trees, which were watered with well water, produced a few peaches per peach tree during the month of June.

The IVO 1 peach trees, which were watered with city water, produced a few peaches per peach tree during the month of June.

The second evaluation: The second evaluation was conducted in June during harvest time. The CO 1 peach trees, which were watered with well water, produced one and half bushels +/- per peach tree during the month of June.

The IVO 1 peach trees, which were watered with city water, produced one bushel +/- per peach tree during the month of June.

The third evaluation: The third evaluation was conducted in June during harvest time. The CO 1 produced two bushels +/- of peaches per peach tree during the month of June.

The IVO 1 also produced two bushels +/- per peach tree during the month of June.

Conclusion: I planted the peach trees in CO 1 and IVO 1 after the winter solstice of December 21. Next, I fertilized the CO 1 and IVO 1 peach trees with the same fertilizer and amount in early spring. I kept fertilizing the peach trees throughout the spring and summer the first year and subsequent years. The fertilizer I used was Southern AG All-Purpose Fertilizer (10 10 10) because it has the essential nitrogen, phosphorus, and potassium to support plant root growth, support crown growth, increase crop yield, support disease resistance, and enhance water preservation.

The number 10 of the fertilizer means it contains 10 percent of the pound weight of the bag for each mineral in the fertilizer bag. Another good reason why I chose (10 10 10) fertilizer was because it is mild; therefore, when it was applied on peach trees, the leaves do not scorch during high-temperature days. I always water the peach trees right after I fertilize them. The All Purpose Fertilizer (10 10 10) can be purchased at a farm supply store and on the Web.

A practical reason why the first and second evaluation the peach trees of CO 1 were taller, trunks were thicker, and produced more peaches than IVO 1 was because the CO 1 trees were watered with well water, which had minerals and nutrients, while the IVO 1 peach trees were watered with city water, which didn't have significant minerals and nutrients except for some chlorine. Although since both the CO 1 and IVO 1 were fertilized with the same kind and amount of fertilizer throughout the two-year-and-six-month experiment, the IVO 1 peach trees caught up with the CO 1, and both the IVO 1 and CO 1 grew about the same height; their tree trunks were approximately the same thickness, and both the CO 1 and IVO 1 produced approximately the same amount of peaches by the third evaluation.

Planting Tall and Short Peach Trees

Preparing and Planting Tall and Short Peach Trees

After the winter solstice in December 21 occurred, I planted six-feet-plus tall bare-root peach trees in the controlled peach CO 2 and four-feet bare-root short peach trees in the experimental peach trees in IVO 2. I then trimmed off the limbs of the experimental IVO 2 peach trees and only left the main stem of the trees planted in the ground.

Since the four-feet short peach trees limbs were all trimmed off, they didn't produce peaches the first evaluation during harvesttime in June and July. Refer to figure 2 to see a trimmed short four-feet peach tree without limbs. Although the short peach trees' limbs were trimmed off, the short peach trees grew back very rapidly because they received the appropriate amount of minerals, nutrients, water, and radiant energy from the sun.

As the trees grew, I continued to train four-feet bare-root short peach trees new limbs by trimming the limbs into the shape of a bowl, and the tree limbs were approximately five feet from ground level. The purpose for training the short trees' limbs in a bowl shape was so that the peaches growing in the bowl area could receive maximum direct radiant energy from the sun, and the peach trees had good air circulation; thus, more peaches would ripen faster.

After experiment 2 was conducted, I did my best to prune and train the six-to-nine-feet-tall tree in CO 2 into five-feet-to-six-feet bowl-shape trees the best way possible so that the peaches could receive radiant energy from the sun and fresh air. Therefore, in subsequent years, these bare-root six-feet-plus-tall trees produced more healthy peaches. Refer to figure 3 that illustrates a nine-feet-tall peach tree trained into a six-feet bowl-shaped tree.

As a general rule, a healthy three-year-old-plus short bare-root-trained peach tree produces from three to six bushels of peaches per year. A peach tree can grow as tall as fifteen feet plus if it is not pruned and/or trimmed. The best time that I did some heavy pruning of the tall peach trees was at the end of fall and the beginning of winter, which is in December 21. I also did some light pruning during the summer months, and this is all right to do during this time.

The peach trees can live for approximately twenty years plus, providing they are nurtured properly. Sometimes peach trees don't produce healthy, delicious peaches because they are not pruned and/ or fertilized properly. Also, the peach trees have been known not to produce peaches due to lack of chilling hours.

Education Experiment 2

The Purpose for Conducting This Experiment

This experiment was conducted to determine if the trained four-feet bare-root short peach trees in IVO 2 produced more healthy peaches than the six-feet bare-root plus tall peach trees in the CO 2 at the end of the three-and-a-half-year experiment.

Criteria for Conducting Experiment 2

The peach tree variety selected for the experiment was Loring.

The number and the size of peach trees used for CO 2: There were ten six-feet-tall bare-root trees used for this experiment.

The number and the size of peach trees used for IVO 2: There were ten four-feet short bare-root trees used for the experiment.

Fertilizer: The CO 2 and IVO 2 peach trees were fertilized with the same fertilizer, which was the Multipurpose 10 10 10, and the same amount was applied to each peach tree.

Water: The CO 2 and IVO 2 peach trees were watered with well water. The city water was not used for IVO 2 to conduct this experiment.

Experiment duration: three-and-a-half years.

Evaluations: Four evaluations were conducted to determine if the trimmed and trained four-feet-short peach trees in the IVO 2 produced more peaches than the six-feet-tall peach trees in the CO 2 by the fourth evaluation. The evaluations were conducted in June at the beginning of harvest period.

The first evaluation in June: The CO 2 and IVO 2 peach trees were planted right after December 21 when the winter solstice started. Then six months later in the month of June, the first evaluation was conducted. The six-feet-tall bare-root peach trees of CO 2 produced a few peaches per tree, but the four-feet-short bare-root trees of IVO 2 didn't produce any peaches because their limbs were trimmed off, so when the limbs grew again, they could be trained to grow in a bowl shape.

The second evaluation in June: The CO 2 peach trees produced a bushel + or – of peaches per tree. The IVO 2 peach trees produced a few peaches per tree.

The third evaluation in June: The CO 2 peach trees produced one and a half bushels + or - of peaches per tree, and the IVO 2 peach trees produced one and a half bushels + or - of peaches per tree.

The fourth evaluation in June: The CO 2 tree produced two bushels + or –, and the IVO 2 peach trees produced three bushels + or -.

Conclusion: The experiment showed that the trimmed and trained four-feet-short bare-root peach trees of IVO 2 produced more healthy peaches than the six-feet-tall bare-root peach trees in the CO 2 by the fourth evaluation. The reason why the IVO 2 peach trees produced more healthy peaches than the CO 2 trees was because the IVO 2 trees were properly trimmed and trained to grow five feet high + or - in a bowl shape so that the peaches could receive maximum radiant energy from the sun and fresh air. In addition, the minerals, nutrients, and water could be dispersed throughout the five-feet trees more easily.

In conclusion, the experiment shows that it is best to plant four-feet bare-root short peach trees than plant six-feet bare-root trees because four-feet trained trees will produce more healthy peaches in four years, providing the peach grower is willing to wait four years. Refer to figure 4 to observe a bowl-shape mature-trained peach tree.

After the experiment was conducted, I trimmed and trained the CO 2 peach trees the best I could, and the peach trees produced healthier and more peaches in subsequent years.

Planting, Fertilizing, and Pollenating the Peach Trees

Planting Peach Trees

There are some peach tree growers who believe that it is best not to fertilize the planting holes where the peach trees are going to be planted after the winter solstice, which is on December 21. One of the main reasons is that by fertilizing the peach trees they might leaf out early during a winter freeze, killing the newly planted peach trees. By the same token, there are other peach tree growers who feel that some fertilizer should be placed in the planting holes because the peach trees need nutrition when planted to help them grow into healthy trees. Since I planted the peach tree in winter, I was afraid that the peach trees would leaf out during a freeze that would harm the trees; therefore, I chose not to fertilize the peach trees when I planted them. After I planted the peach tree, none of the peach trees leafed out early, and all the peach trees survived to be fertilized in the spring when I fertilized the peach trees.

Another area of concern that an individual should understand is that when planting the peach trees in winter, he or she should not plant the trees if the weather temperature is below 32 F degrees. The individual should wait until the weather is going to be above freezing for several days. If there is not a window of good weather during the early part of winter, then the individual can plant the peach trees in the latter days of winter. If the peach trees are planted below 32 F degrees, the tender peach tree roots will be damaged, and the peach trees could expire.

Since the location of the peach planting sites A and B were close to some pine trees, I checked the soil if it was too acidic. If the pH was 7+, I added some agriculture lime around the planted peach trees. I also trim the crowns of the peach trees into a shape of a bowl so that the peaches could receive the radiant energy from the sun, and since the trees were shorter, they could obtain sufficient water, nutrients, and minerals.

Fertilizing Peach Trees

I planted the peach trees after the winter solstice; I applied the Southern AG All-Purpose Fertilizer (10 10 10) on the peach trees because it has the essential elements, which are nitrogen (N), phosphate (PO 4), and potash (K2O), which make the peach trees grow well. I placed the fertilizer around the peach tree trunks after the vernal equinox, which starts on March 21, which is the first day of spring, because it is best to fertilize when the peach trees show activities such as flowering.

The amount of fertilizer that was applied on the peach trees was an 8 oz. cup for every inch in diameter of the peach tree trunk. Since the young peach trees' trunks were one inch + or − in diameter, I applied an 8 oz. cup of All Purpose Fertilizer (10-10-10) around the trunks of the peach trees in the month of March. Then in May,

I repeated the same fertilization regimen I used in late March to give the peach trees a boost before harvest in June.

After the harvest, I applied another 8 oz. cup of all-purpose (10 10 10) around the trunk of the trees in the month of August before the dormant stage of the autumnal equinox that started on September 22. Each time I fertilized the peach trees, I watered the trees until the fertilizer soaked into the tree roots so nutrients could be absorbed by the peach trees' roots to be dispersed throughout the peach tree crowns.

As a general rule, the peach trees do not require too much fertilizer unless the soil that the trees are planted in is deficient in minerals and nutrients. When the peach tree trunks increased to 2 inches in diameter +/or -, I increased the amount of fertilizer to two cups, and this equaled to 16 ounces; and whenever the peach tree trunks grew another inch, I added another 8 oz. cup of fertilizer.

I continued to fertilize and water the trees in the subsequent years and used the same time schedule to fertilize. The All Purpose Fertilizer (10-10-10) is sold in most feed and farm supply stores and on the Web.

Pollination of the Peach Trees

Most peach trees are self-fertilized, such as the Elberta and Loring, and are good peach trees to cross-pollinate with Alamar, Candoka, Halberta, and Mikado, which are cross-pollenating peach trees. However, the cross-pollinating J. H. Hale peach trees will not cross-pollenate with the Elberta tree. As a general rule, peach trees produce more peaches if the honeybees pollenate them, but if bees are not available, the self-pollenating and cross-pollinating peach trees will still produce peaches, but not as many.

The US Department of Agriculture List of Minerals

A List of Minerals and the Matching Deficiencies of the Minerals

The following is the list of minerals with the corresponding symptoms that are created when a peach tree is deficient of any of these minerals. Therefore, I observed my peach trees for any of these symptoms.

If I were to spot a symptom on a peach tree, I would match it with the corresponding mineral. I would then purchase the mineral and apply it on the peach tree according to the mineral application directions.

1. Boron: The peach tree leaves become dark green, the bark starts oozing gum, and the lateral buds break, giving a "witch broom" appearance.
2. Calcium: The peach trees will have die back, tree growth is reduced, and leaf drop occurs.
3. Copper: The peach tree leaves turn dark green, with young irregular leaves becoming long and narrow, and severe wilting of the leaves occurs.
4. Iron: If the peach tree has an iron deficiency, the leaves could obtain interveinal chlorosis, which will cause defoliation of the leaves.
5. Nitrogen: The peach tree growth stops as leaves first become pale then assume a reddish tint, and the trees produce less fruit.
6. Magnesium: The peach tree's root system and fruit buds are reduced.
7. Manganese: The peach tree's leaves become dull, yellowish-green, and stunted, with terminal growth ensuing.
8. Phosphorus: The peach tree's leaves become dark green to purple, and the tree will have early defoliation.
9. Zinc: The lack of zinc in peach trees, the leaves are mottling then they become small, narrow, and pointed with wavy

margins, after which time chlorosis occurs. Defoliation then ensues. There are also deposits of gummy material on the roots.

How Minerals, Nutrients, and Water Are Dispersed

How Minerals, Nutrients, and Water Are Dispersed Throughout the Peach Tree

Botany teaches us that the peach tree uses two ways to distribute minerals, nutrients, and water throughout the tree. The cambium is located between the xylem and phloem. The purpose for the cambium is to promote growth of the xylem and phloem by producing vascular tissue for increasing the need to conduct food and water to tissues formed due to the new tree growth.

As per the xylem, its function is to transport water and minerals from the roots to the stem and leaves of the peach tree. The xylem also provides physical support to the tissues and organs so that the plant doesn't bend. The xylem tissue consists of a variety of specialized water-conducting cells. The xylem forms a continuous hollow tube, and it is strengthened by a chemical called lignin and tube cells. The minerals, nutrients, and water flow from the roots in an upward flow to the crown of the tree.

The third part is called the phloem. Its function is to collect photoassimilates (ions, amino acids, hormones, and other molecules) in green leaves and distribute them throughout the peach tree. The phloem also transports sucrose and nutrients within the tree that are produced in the tree leaves during the photosynthesis process. The minerals, nutrients, and water flow up and down the phloem basically to feed the green parts to the peach tree.

As per plant science, one of the differences between plant and animal is that the plant cells can make their own food to live through a process called photosynthesis, but an animal has to eat another animal and/or plant to survive. In addition, the plants evolved on planet Earth long before the animals and mammals evolved.

Four Common Fungi That Are Harmful to Peach Trees

Armillaria Root Rot and Honey Fungus

When I was selecting the location to plant the peach trees, I made sure the location did not have any oak trees growing nearby sites A and B because one of the fungi that oak trees acquire is the Armillaria root rot fungus that will invade the peach tree roots rapidly and will kill the tree. This fungus is the second-worst fungus in the United States. I read about the Armillaria fungus on how devastating this fungus can be to peach trees in *Southeastern Peach Grower's Handbook*, the Cooperative Extension Service, the University of Georgia College of Agricultural and Environmental Sciences, Athens.

Scientific name: *Armillaria mellea*

Common name: Armillaria root rot and honey fungus

Transmitted: Armillaria spreads by any activity that moves soil containing infested wood fragments.

Cause: Armillaria root rot is caused by several species of the fungus Armillaria that colonizes the roots and the base of the trunk, which causes wood decay. Overwatering might cause Armillaria to manifest in the roots of the peach trees.

Symptoms: A mottling peach tree indicates it has been infected with a fungus such as *Armillaria* fungus, especially when honey-colored mushrooms grow close to the mottling tree and the tree has decay on the lower part of its trunk. Another way to confirm that the fungus is *Armillaria* fungus is that it has white fan-shaped mycelia, thin, flat sheets of fungal tissue that grow just below the bark. To find these mycelial fans, one would have to dig into the soil at the base of the trunk and down to twelve-plus inches beneath the soil line. Then with a knife cut away the dead bark of a large root to reveal the mycelial fans and rotted wood. This is a common symptom of *Armillaria* root rot. Other visible symptoms at the surface include flat cankers on the trunk or main stem near the ground which causes bleeding sap which is called gummosis. Other symptoms that indicate that the mottling peach tree has a fungus is when it has discolored foliage, reduced growth, diebacks, and diseased leaves that turn gray and appear powdery.

Control: Plant science states that one of the best ways to control fungi is not to overwater the peach tree and to provide good water drainage for the peach tree. It is difficult to spray fungicide on *Armillaria* root rot fungus because it has some mycelial fans that are hidden under the bark and enclosed in a protective envelope. Since the mottling peach tree which has the Armillaria fungus will eventually expire, then there is no harm in applying the homemade remedy to try to extend the life of the mottling peach tree. If the peach tree grower decides to use the remedy, then the peach tree roots need to be checked to see if the peach tree has some white firm roots because without them the peach tree will not survive. If indeed the peach tree has some white firm roots, then the Homemade Organic Fungicide Liquid Mixture Remedy (HOFLMR) can be applied to extend the life of the mottling peach tree, providing the remedy works. It is left up to the peach tree grower to decide whether to apply or not apply this remedy on mottling peach trees.

The remedy I used to control fungi was a homemade organic fungicide liquid mixture remedy (HOFLMR). First, I soaked the mottling peach tree roots with water. Second, I poured organic fungicide Organocide 3-in-1 Garden Spray concentrate into a five-gallon bucket and mixed it with water according to manufacturer's instruction. Third, I added five cups of All Purpose Fertilizer (10-10-10) into the liquid mixture. Fourth, I poured the mixture on the mottling peach tree roots and lightly watered the roots again in order for the fungicide mixture to soak into the roots. I don't apply this remedy to a fruiting mottling tree, and I only use an organic fungicide concentrate to make the organic liquid mixture remedy. The remedy may be repeated when it appears that the mottling tree needs an extra treatment to survive. I have had some success by applying this remedy only to extend the life of the mottling peach tree but not to cure it.

Brown Root Rot Fungus

The brown root rot fungus invades mainly the young peach tree roots that are one to seven years old.

Scientific name: *Phellinus noxius*

Common name: Brown root rot fungus

Transmitted: When the soil is soggy, the brown root rot fungus spores multiply, and the fungus starts to spread rapidly throughout the root system of the peach tree. The brown root rot fungus also spreads through root contact, contaminated soil, ground water, and even shoe soles can be contaminated with brown root rot fungus.

Cause: Brown root rot fungus is caused by *Phellinus noxius*. This fungus invades the tree roots, causing decay. When this happens, it cuts off water and nutrient supply to the crown of the tree, causing the demise of the peach tree.

Symptoms: The brown root rot fungus will invade the peach tree root system There are some signs that indicate that a mottling peach tree has brown root rot fungus which are brown mushy roots, wilting, and yellow leaves. When the mottling peach tree has brown mushy roots it cuts off the nutrients and water supply of the peach tree which will expire the tree. Other symptoms that indicate brown root rot fungus could have invaded the peach tree are diebacks, distorted leaves, and slow growth of the mottling peach tree. All these maladies will eventually cause the demise of the mottling peach tree if it is not treated for pests.

Control: Plant science teaches that there isn't a cure for brown root fungus once it infects a peach tree. Furthermore, there are a few ways to control brown root rot fungus. One of the ways to control fungi on peach trees is by exercising the usual and customary way of not overwatering the peach because it creates a soggy condition that prevents roots from absorbing oxygen which is required to live. If this happens, the roots will die and decay, and their rot will infect the healthy peach tree roots. Another way to prevent fungi is to provide good water drainage for the peach tree especially when it rains. The decayed limbs, peaches, twigs, and debris that fall on the ground should be picked up and taken to the burn pile or barrel. This is a good way to stop spreading fungi and other pests in the orchard.

Next, the mottling tree root system needs to be checked out to see if any of the roots are brown and mushy and/or white and firm. If all the roots are brown and mushy then the mottling trees will expire soon. Therefore, the mottling peach tree needs to be dug out with its roots and contaminated soil that was around the rotten roots and taken to the burn pile. The planting hole should be sprayed with a nonorganic fungicide that has metallic copper and filled with new fresh soil. However, if the mottling peach tree has some brown mushy roots and some rich white firm roots then the mottling trees has an opportunity to live longer. The brown mushy roots along with their contaminated soil need to be taken to the burn pile but leaving the rich white firm roots in the planting hole, then filling the hole with fresh new soil and adding some water to the planting hole for new root growth.

At this juncture, the peach tree grower has the choice of whether or not to apply the HOFLMR on the mottling peach tree that only has some rich white firm roots. If the HOFLMR is applied, then there is a possibility that the mottling tree might live longer than usual but there is no guarantee.

Brown Rot

Another fungus that invades the peach tree is the brown rot. The brown rot is observed in the spring when the pink blooms of the peach turn to mush and die. The fungus also forms grayish fussy spore mass on the peach tree branch, forming a fuzzy canker, and jellylike gel starts coming out of the limbs and peaches.

Scientific name: *Monolinia fructicola*

Common name: Brown rot

Cause: Brown Rot is caused by *Monolinia fructicola*. The brown rot fungus survives the winter in a mummified fruit, which is on the ground, on the tree, in a twig, and in a branch canker.

Transmitted: The brown rot spores overwinter in shriveled fruit, infected twigs, and branches. In the spring, the fungus manifests in cool, wet conditions and produces spores. The spores then spread to blossoms by rain, wind, and insects. If the peach blossoms are wet, the spores will accumulate on the blossoms, and the brown rot infects the peach tree blossoms before they are pollinated. When this happens, the blossoms die and fall off the peach trees.

Symptoms: The peach trees' pink blossoms turn brown, die, and fall off the peach trees before being pollinated. The peaches that might be pollinated and stay on the tree may turn gray due to the accumulation of spores of the peach. Brown rot is not generally a deadly disease to the peach trees, but once the brown rot invades the fruit, there isn't a cure to keep the peach fruit from rotting.

Control: If the peach tree were to be infected with brown rot the premature dead peach blooms spores peaches, and canker develop in the twigs therefore they should be removed immediately and burned at the burn pile or barrel. Next spray all the peach tree with a non-organic fungicide that has metallic copper that is suggested by the county extension agent. Then the mottling peach tree needs to be pruned to control the brown rot from spreading to other peach trees in the orchard. The peach tree grower may apply the HOFLMR on the peach tree if he decides to apply it. The peach grower can apply the HOFLMR whenever there is an opportunity to apply it. The HOFLMR is a remedy so it will only extend the peach tree life of the mottling tree if the remedy works.

To control root rot and other pests, the Organic Neem Oil Concentrate can be sprayed on all the peach trees in the fall. The neem oil will destroy the pests that manifest in the dry peaches, dry twigs, and dry limbs that are left hanging on the peach tree. If this organic product is applied in the fall then there will be fewer pests in the spring.

Peach Scab

Another fungus that is harmful to peach trees is the peach scab, which is sometimes known as "freckles" because the small black spots are all over the peaches. The black spots are about one-fourth-inch in diameter, and it has velvety dark spot cracks.

Scientific name: *Cladoposium carpophilum*

Common name: Peach scab and freckles

Transmitted: By spores spread by rain, wind, and insects

Cause: The peach scab overwinters in twigs and limbs that were infected the previous year. During spring and summer, large numbers of microscopic spores create twig lesions. The spores remain attached to the twig until they become moistened. Then when the spores are moistened, they are spread by splashing rain or the wind to developing peaches.

Symptoms: The peach scab are small, round, olive-colored spots that develop on the peach. As these spots develop, they enlarge and merge to become odd-shaped dark-green or black blotches on the peach. The peaches that are severely infected may be cracked or stunted.

Control: If the peach trees acquire peach scab by observing infected twigs, then remove them immediately and burn the twigs at the burn pile or barrel. Next, spray the peach trees that has peach scab with a feri-lome open-end sprayer with a non-organic fungicide that has copper that was suggested by the county extension agent. Then spray all the peach trees with Organic Neem Oil Concentrate fungicide in the fall with a ferti-lome hose-end sprayer to kill the scab that were left in the twigs of the peach trees. Organic Neem Oil Concentrate solution is an all-season pesticide that controls bacteria, fungi, and insects.

The HOFLMR can be applied to the mottling peach tree because the peach scab sometimes invades the peach tree roots. This remedy can only extend the life of the mottling tree if the remedy works.

Education Experiment 3

Purpose for Conducting Education Experiment 3

The purpose for conducting experiment 3 was to determine if using program 1, which sprays nonorganic pesticides to control insects and fungi on site A CO 3 peach trees, is more effective for controlling pests than using program 2, which sprays organic pesticides on the site B IVO 3 peach trees.

Spraying Programs 1 and 2 Spraying Stages

Stage 1: Spraying the site A CO 3 and site B IVO 3 ground surfaces.

Program 1: Spray the site A CO 3 ground surface weeds by using one of the county extension agent's nonorganic suggested herbicides. A ferti-lome hose-end sprayer is used to spray the CO 3 ground surface.

Program 2: Spray the site B IVO 3 ground surface weeds by using Concentrate Weed and Grass Killer by Eco Living Solutions. A ferti-lome hose end sprayer was used to spray the IVO 3 ground surface.

Stage 2: Green tip stage

Program 1: Sprayed the site A CO 3 peach trees' green tips were sprayed with a suggested county extension's agent nonorganic insecticide when the blossoms' green tips appear in spring. A ferti-lome hose-end sprayer was used to spray the peach blossom green tips before they opened.

Program 2: Sprayed the site B IVO 3 peach trees green tips with organic Organocide Concentrate insecticide and fungicide because fungicide is included in the Organocide. A ferti-lome hose-end sprayer was used to spray the peach blossom green tips before they opened.

Stage 3: Pre-blossom stage

Program 1: Spray the site A CO 3 peach trees when the pre-blossoms showed full color before opening. The peach trees were sprayed with suggested county extension agent's nonorganic fungicide that could include copper because copper controls fungi very well. A ferti-lome hose-end sprayer was used to spray the CO 3 peach trees.

Program 2: Spray the site B IVO 3 peach trees when the pre-blossoms show full color before opening. The peach trees were sprayed with organic Organocide concentrate. A ferti-lome hose-end sprayer was used to spray the IVO 3 peach trees.

Stage 4: Blossom stage

Program 1: When the site A CO 3 peach trees blossomed, they were not sprayed with no kind of pesticide because it might get into the blossom and disrupt the pollination and fertilization process being conducted in the peach blossoms and no peaches will be produced. Therefore, peach blossoms should never be sprayed inside the blossoms because peaches will not be produced.

Program 2: When the site B IVO 3 peach trees blossomed, they were not sprayed with no kind of pesticides because it will disrupt the pollination and fertilization process being conducted in the peach blossom and no peaches will be produced. Therefore, the peach blossoms should never be sprayed inside the blossoms because peaches will not be produced.

During this blossom stage, it is a good time to thin the blossoms so that the peaches will grow larger because there will be less competition for nutrients and water. The blossoms were not thinned because in Northeast Texas there are several freezing windstorms during spring that will naturally thin the blossoms of the peach trees. In the event the blossoms need to be thinned, it can be done by rubbing blossoms from the undersides of the branches by hand or with the aid of a brush but retain blossoms on branch tops.

Stage 5: Petal fall stage

Program 1: When the site A CO 3 peach trees blossoms petal fall occurred, the peach trees were sprayed with the county extension agent's suggested nonorganic insecticide. The peach trees were wet-sprayed with a ferti-lome handheld sprayer during this stage because the reproduction process of the peaches might not be completed.

Program 2: When the site B IVO 3 peach tree blossoms petals fall occurred, the peach trees were wet-spot sprayed with a ferti-lome handheld sprayer during this stage because the reproduction process of the peaches might not be completed. Organicide was used to spray the peach trees.

Stage 6: Shuck (blossom) fall stage

Program 1: When the site A CO 3 peach trees shuck fall occurred, the peach trees were sprayed with the county extension agent's suggested nonorganic insecticide. A ferti-lome hose-end sprayer was used to spray the insecticide.

Program 2: When the site B IVO 3 peach trees shuck fall occurred, the peach trees were sprayed with Organocide Concentrate to control insecticide and fungicide because Organocide includes fungicide. A ferti-lome hose-end sprayer was used to spray IVO 3.

Stage 7: In early-April peach-tree-spraying stage

Program 1: In early April, the peach trees in site A CO 3 were sprayed with a fungicide that could include copper, and the fungicide was suggested in the material provided by the county extension agent. A ferti-lome hose-end sprayer was used to spray the CO 3 with fungicide.

Program 2: Early April, the peach trees in site B IVO 3 were sprayed with organic Organocide insecticide and fungicide. A ferti-lome hose-end sprayer was used to spray the peach trees.

Stage 8: Early-May peach-tree-spraying stage

Program 1: In early May, the peach trees in site A CO 3 were sprayed with a nonorganic insecticide suggested by the county extension agent. The reason why the peach trees were sprayed in early May was because it allowed approximately three weeks before harvest time in June in order for the nonorganic insecticide to dissipate. A ferti-lome hose sprayer was used to spray the nonorganic insecticide.

Program 2: In early May, the peach trees in site B IVO 3 were sprayed with Organocide insecticide and fungicide. A ferti-lome hose-end sprayer was used to spray the IVO 3.

Stage 9: Harvest stage
Program 1: The CO 3 peach trees were not sprayed during the harvest stage because the nonorganic insecticide or fungicide might remain on the peach skin that might be eaten by consumers. As a general rule, the peach tree farmers stop spraying the peach trees approximately three weeks before picking the peaches to eat and/or sell.

Program 2: Although the Organocide concentrate is organic, the peach trees in IVO 3 were not sprayed during this time because Organocide is still considered to be an insecticide and fungicide that kill insects and fungi. Therefore, if it kills pests, it could also be mildly harmful for humans to eat.

Stage 10: Predormant stage
Program 1: The CO 3 peach trees were sprayed with a nonorganic pesticide suggested by the county extension agent during August in order to control insects and fungi especially the bores that manifest during this time. I sprayed the insecticide and fungicide with a ferti-lome open-end sprayer.

Program 2: The IVO 3 peach trees were sprayed with Neem Max Concentrate in early August in order to control the insects and fungi, and especially the bores that manifest during this time. Since neem oil is an all-season insecticide and fungicide, I also spray the Neem Max concentrate after the first freeze and leaf fall, which is right before dormancy on the IVO 3 peach trees. Neem Max Concentrate will control the overwintered insects and hatching eggs of the pests. Thus, the peach trees should not have leaf curl and other fungal diseases in the forthcoming spring. A ferti-lome hose-end sprayer was used to spray the organic pesticide.

The peach tree variety used: Loring peach trees

The number and height trees used to conduct experiment 3: There were ten six-feet bare-root peach trees used for CO 3. There were ten six-feet bare-root peach trees used for IVO 3.

Evaluation

Three yearly evaluations during harvest time in June.

First evaluation: Since the peach trees were planted after the winter solstice in December 21, the peach trees had been planted for approximately five months. The CO 3 and IVO 3 peach trees didn't produce enough peaches to determine if the CO 3 peaches were healthier than the IVO 3 peaches during the harvest month of June.

Second evaluation: When I compared the CO 3 peaches with the IVO 3 peaches during the harvest month of June, the CO 3 peaches' skins were healthier than the IVO 3 peaches'. The IVO 3 peaches had some skin discoloration, and they had some insects that had bored into the exocarp of the peaches. The IVO 3 peaches continue to have the customary strong peach perfume aroma and peach taste, but the CO 3 peach trees' perfume aroma and peach taste were not as strong as the IVO 3 peaches.

Third evaluation: When I compared the CO 3 peaches with the IVO 3 peaches during the peach harvest month of June, the CO 3 peaches continued to have a healthier skin than the IVO 3 peaches because the IVO 3 peaches had some blemishes, dark spots, and insects that bored into the exocarps of the peaches. The IVO 3 peaches continued to have the strong peach perfume aroma and the peach taste. As per the CO 3 peaches, their peach perfume aroma and taste were not as strong as the IVO 3 peaches.

Conclusion: Experiment 3 concluded that after three evaluations, the CO 3 peaches had better peach skins because the nonorganic solution was more effective for controlling insects and fungi than the organic pesticide. This was the reason why the IVO 3 peaches continued to have blemishes, dark spots, discoloration, and tiny insect larvae in the exocarp of the peaches, although the IVO 3 continued to have a stronger peach perfume aroma and peach taste than the CO 3 peach trees.

Therefore, if the peach consumer chooses the IVO 3 peaches to eat, then he or she will have the option of removing the dark spots, insects, and fungi off the peaches before he or she eats the peaches. In the event a consumer does not remove the pests and accidentally eats the insects, food science teaches that there are basically no ill effects because insects are mostly protein. In fact, there are some companies that are selling insects for human consumption such as the Shop Chirps Products. Peach diseases need to be removed before eating the peach.

Harvesting and Selling Peaches

Harvesting the Peaches in June and July

Basically, the peaches are ripe when the color of the fruit changes from green to yellow. The peaches need to hang on the tree long enough for the flavor and the sugar content to peak, but not too long as the peaches will overripe. Furthermore, once the peaches are picked, they need to be rinsed in cold water to stop any further ripening.

When the peaches are put in half-bushel containers, the stem side should be placed down in the container, and place a newspaper for each layer of peaches. The wholesale price for a half bushel of fresh premium peaches are sold from $40+ per half a bushel, and the nonpremium peaches, referred to as canners, are sold for $20+ per half bushel in Northeast Texas. Some consumers use these nonpremium peaches, which are called canners because they are used for canning. The canners are also used to make peach cobbler and peach pies. If peaches are retailed, the price of the fresh peaches could double the cost of the wholesale price. Most peaches are harvested during June and July, but some varieties are harvested in May and August.

Hobby Lobby sells wood-plank bushel baskets at reasonable prices that are used during harvest time. All kinds and sizes of bushel baskets can be purchased by using the Web.

As a general rule, one pound of peaches equals three medium-sized peaches. Consequently, one bushel contains approximately 150 peaches, and each bushel of peaches weighs between 48 pounds and 52 pounds. If the peaches are sold and transported, they should be placed in certain types of boxes. The boxes should be brought from a company that sells fruit boxes because there are several state laws that regulate what kind of boxes should be used, how the peaches should be placed in the boxes, and how they are transported. Some peach tree farmers claim that the Harvester variety peach is very good to transport because it stays fresh for a longer period of time than most other peach varieties.

Some peach producers have some roadside peach ice cream parlors that are adjacent to their peach orchard where they sell peach ice cream, peaches, and many other peach-related items. This type of domestic business has become very popular and a lucrative business because people love to eat peaches, peach ice cream, peach cobbler, and peach pies.

The *Country World* Magazine

After growing the peaches, I was recognized by reporter Mindy Riffle as being knowledgeable on how to grow the peach trees. She wrote an article in July 29, 2010, about my research entitled "Peach Grower Shares Knowledge," *Country World*, in volume 29, edition 43, 2010. The Web home page is www.CountryWorld. If an individual wants to receive a copy of the article by email, call Melinda at 903-885-8663.

CONCLUSION OF THE PEACH GUIDE

The Role of the Peach Guide

The peach guide was written just in time because food scientists are searching for ways to increase food production in order to feed the increasing population of the world. At present, there are approximately 7.5 billion inhabitants living on planet Earth. The United Nations reports claim there will be approximately 9.7 billion people by 2050.

Americans consume large amounts of food and water, although America's use is justified because America is a self-sustaining agricultural society that exports volumes of food, agricultural technology, equipment, and materials all over the world. Perhaps this is the reason why America is referred to as the "land of milk and honey," but for how much longer is the question.

As per the current Food and Agricultural Organization reports, 11 percent of the Earth's surface is used for growing food, and 70 percent of the Earth's fresh water is used for agriculture. The United States Department of Agriculture (USDA) submits that if everybody in America ate what is recommended, there wouldn't be enough food to feed everybody. In addition, some Americans have a ferocious appetite, causing them to eat the amount of what two or more individuals eat in other countries, and this could cause an increase of food shortage. Therefore, in order to meet the demand of food and obtaining more money for growing more food, intensive farming is being conducted by some food growers to increase food production.

Intensive farming is growing several crops that are being grown on the same soil throughout the year instead growing the crop once a year and plowing the leftover roots, leaves, limbs, and other items back into the soil in order for the soil to continue to keep its vigor with minerals and nutrients from the leftovers' foliage. Furthermore, even if the soil is being fertilized with minerals and nutrients, the soil becomes less nutritional because the humus soil is used up due to excessive use of the soil. Consequently, the structure of the soil will not be able hold enough moisture for growing crops. Thus, without humus soil, the earth's soil ability to filter water and absorb carbon for the food that is grown in the soil will be deficient in minerals and nutrients; thus, the food will be less nutritional.

For example, an individual would have to eat several peaches today in order to obtain the nutrition that one peach had in the year 1950. This humus soil is organic matter that is made of decayed plants and decomposed animals; it takes Mother Earth many years to produce a thin layer of humus soil.

Unfortunately, some soil scientists suspect that the Earth will run out of usable humus soil within sixty years. When this happens, the soil will be so degraded that it will be difficult to grow nutrient-dense food to feed the world's growing population. Perhaps the United States might need to grow its food in countries such as Brazil, Canada, and Venezuela that have abundant amounts of humus soil and ship the food to the United States and other countries that desperately need nutritional food. The Romans used this concept by growing their food in the fertile soil of the Nile River in Egypt and shipping the food to Rome.

Another avenue that can be used to produce additional food is to read this guide to obtain some knowledge on how to grow some homegrown food and apply this knowledge to grow homegrown fruits such as peaches, pears, and plums and apply this knowledge to grow garden veggies. Fortunately, humus organic soil matter can be purchased on the Web. The Web also shows how to make humus soil. Therefore, one can either buy or make a small amount humus soil to grow their own homegrown fruit trees and/or veggies.

At this juncture, the Earth's population is growing at a fast pace, and food is becoming scarce, costly, and less nutritional. Therefore, some individuals who own a patch of land need to consider designating the patch to grow their own homegrown fruits and veggies.

I hope and pray that everybody who reads this peach guide gains some knowledge and understanding on how to grow their own homegrown food in order to supplement their families' and friends' food consumption. If more individuals were to grow some of their own food as the first Americans did, then they could produce enough food to supplement the food supply so there wouldn't be such a huge food shortage, and the United States could continue to be the "cornucopia of the world."

There are words of wisdom that are said among agriculturalist who say, "If there is no agriculture, then there is no civilization, and if there is no civilization, then there are no cities which have schools, churches, libraries, business companies, and government, all of which are vital so that mankind can survive on planet Earth."

SOURCES

- Irrigation-Mart Co.: 200 South Service Road. East Rustin, LA 71270-3442; PH. 318-255-1832
- Texas Department of Agriculture-Pesticide License: 1700 N. Congress, Eleventh Floor; Austin, Texas 78701; Phone number 512-463-7476; Customer Service Ph. 800-835-5832
- Texas Pecan Nursery: 504 Highway. 31 West Chandler, TX 75758; PO Box 306; Chandler, TX 75758; Ph. 903-849-6203; Fax: 903-849-3660; Sales@texaspecannursery.com
- Texas Utility Locator Service: 1410 E. Renner Road. # 100; Richardson, TX 75082; Texas 811.org
- United States Department of Agriculture: 1400 Independence Avenue. SW Washington, DC 20250; Organic Information Ph. 202-720-3252 to learn how to certify organic fruits.

FIGURES

Figure 1. Drawing of a cross section of a peach.

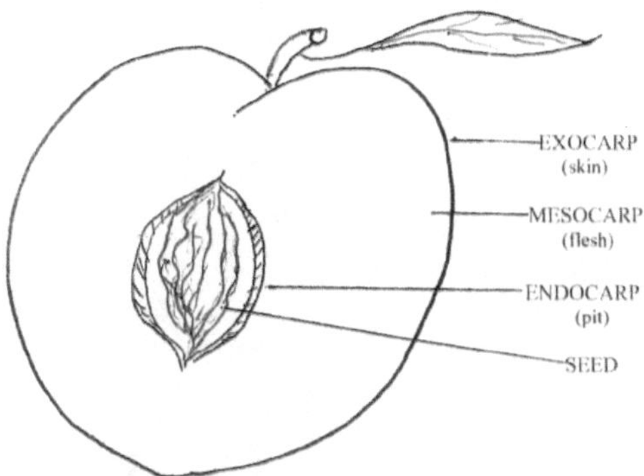

Figure 2. Drawing on how to trim a peach tree after planting it in order to train it into a bowl-shape tree.

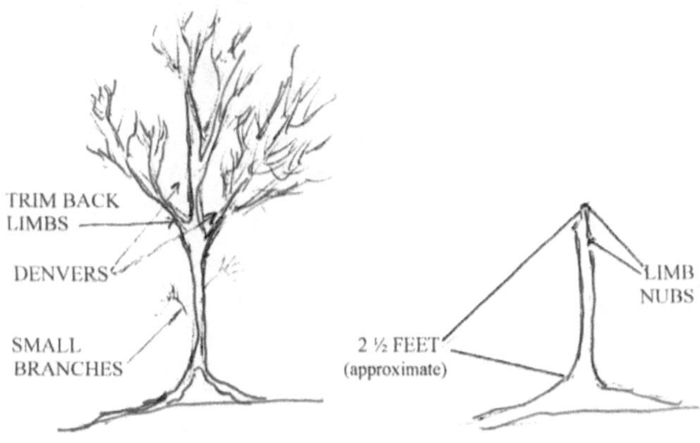

Figure 3. Drawing of how to trim a tree to become a bowl-shape trained tree.

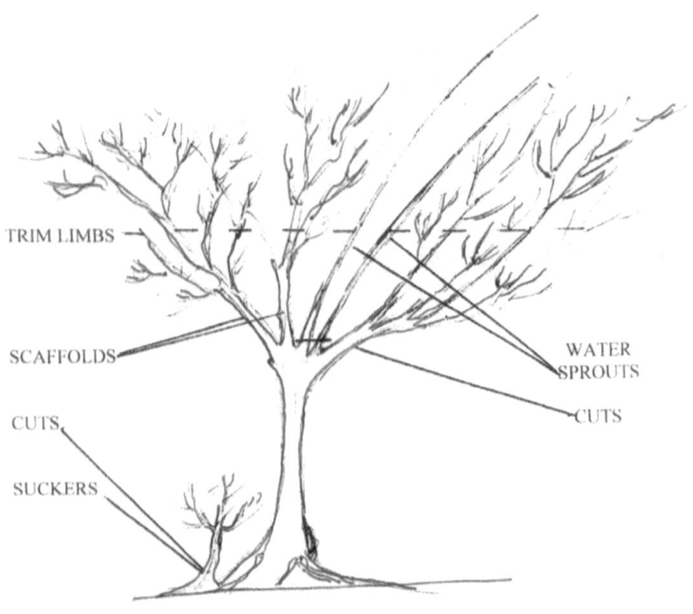

Figure 4. Drawing of a bowl-shape trained peach tree.

GLOSSARY

annual broadleaves. Plants that live for only one season.

acid. It's any substance that in water solution tastes sour, changes a base blue litmus paper to an acid red, reacts with some metals to liberate hydrogen to promote chemical reactions (acid catalysis), and reacts with the bases to form salts.

alkaline. It is an alkali basic and ionic salt of an alkali metal. An alkali can also be defined as a base that dissolves in water. Thus, alkalis are bases, but not all bases are alkalis. Some of the water-soluble bases are NaOH and KOH. A solution of a soluble base has a pH greater than 7.0. Alkalis are very corrosive in nature.

all-purpose fertilizer 10 10 10. It is used for fertilizing shrubs and trees. It contains 10 percent of the pound weight of the bag for each nutrient. The nutrients are nitrogen (N) 10 percent, phosphate (P205) 10 percent, and potash (K20) 10 percent.

base. A base is a substance that will neutralize an acid but does not dissolves in water. A base will also turn acid red litmus to paper blue. All alkali are bases but not all bases are alkali. Some examples of bases that are not alkali are copper oxide, ferrous oxide, and zinc carbonate.

bacteria. Small single-celled organisms, and the body is full of bacteria.

bacterium. The singular form of the plural word *bacteria*. It is also a member of a large group of unicellular microorganisms that have cell walls but lack organelles and an organized nucleus, including some that can cause disease.

bare-root peach tree. Is a tree that is not placed in a plant pot, or the roots are not wrapped in a burlap sack that is made ready to sell but instead it is sold completely bare root, which generally costs less.

biodegradable. A substance capable of being decomposed by bacteria or other living organisms.

botany. Is a study of plants including their ecology, genetics, physiology, and structure.

bug. A bug is a particular insect that is distinguished by having mouthparts that are modified for piercing and sucking into peaches.

canker. It's a destructive fungal disease of fruit trees; it also invades tree bark, and poor soil may cause the peach trees to have canker.

chlorophyll. It's a green pigment that is present in green plants that is responsible for the absorption of light to provide energy for photosynthesis.

chlorosis. Is the yellowing of leaves caused by a lack of chlorophyll.

coliform bacteria. It's defined as rod-shaped non-spore forming bacteria that can ferment lactose with the production of acid and gas when incubated at 35–37 °C. Coliform bacteria is harmful because it is the feces of all warm-blooded animals.

cornucopia. It's a symbol of plenty consisting of a goat's horn overflowing with flowers, fruit, and corn.

cultivate. It means to prepare and use land for crops or gardening.

deciduous. The peach tree sheds its leaves annually.

dieback. A condition in which a peach tree begins to die from the tip of its leaves to the limbs due to a disease and/or an unfavorable environment

dormant. It's when plants prepare their soft tissues for freezing temperatures, dry weather, or water and nutrient shortage during the winter months to be used during mild climate.

elliptic. It's having the shape of an ellipse, which is an elongated circle, stretched into an oval.

empirical. It's verifiable by observation and/or experience rather than theory.

fall equinox. Is the nickname of "autumnal equinox," which occurs on September 22. This is when fall starts in the Northern Hemisphere and it is spring in the Southern Hemisphere.

forage. It's bulky food such as grass or hay for cattle.

fungi. It's the plural of *fungus*, which is a member of the eukaryotic organisms that are yeasts and molds. The fungi belongs to a different kingdom from plants and bacteria.

fungus. It's the singular of *fungi*.

heel-in. It's to temporarily plant the roots of a tree or trees in one hole with soil before planting them permanently.

herbaceous weeds. They are vascular plants that have no woody stems above ground, including perennials and annuals.

hybrid. A hybrid peach tree is a cross-bred peach that is a result of the breeders cross-pollinating two unrelated peach tree species.

independent variable. It is a variable that stands alone.

insect. It's a small invertebrate animal that has six legs and generally one or two pairs of wings.

lanceolate. Refers to a leaf that is wider at the base than at the midpoint, tapers toward the apex, and has a length-to-width ratio of 3:1.

leaf out. Refers to sprout and open leaves.

mesocarp. Refers to the middle layer of the pericarp of a fruit that is between the endocarp and the exocarp.

mineral. It is a solid chemical compound with a fairly well-defined chemical composition and a specific crystal structure that occurs naturally.

mottle. Trees that mottle consists of yellowish spots on tree leaves that is a sign of a disease and/or malnutrition that if not treated in time will cause the tree to expire.

necrosis. Means the death of cells in plants due to disease.

Nemaguard rootstock. Is highly resistant to root knot nematodes, and it is also drought tolerant, promotes growth, and repels diseases.

nematodes. Is any worm of the large phylum Nematoda, such as roundworms. Nematodes are among the most abundant animals on earth.

nurture. It is to care for, feed, train, protect, encourage the growth and development of the peach tree.

parasite. It's an organism that lives in or on an organism of another and benefits by deriving nutrients at the other's expense.

perennials. Are plants that come back up from their roots every year in the spring.

pink lady. It's the common name for spring pink bloom of the peach tree.

pH. The pH is a measure of the acidity or base of water. The range goes from 0 to 14, with 7 being neutral. If the pH is less than 7, it indicates acidity, and a pH greater than 7 indicates a base. The pH measures the amount of free hydrogen and hydroxyl ions in the water.

phloem. It's the vascular tissue in peach trees that conducts sugars and other metabolic products made in leaves during photosynthesis downward from the leaves to areas where it is needed in the tree.

photosynthesis. Is a process by which green plants use sunlight to synthesize foods from carbon dioxide and water. Photosynthesis in plants uses the green pigment chlorophyll to generate oxygen.

quiescence. It's the resting stage in normal or nondormant peach trees waiting for the right condition to happen before the trees bloom. Such as the buds of the peach trees bloom when the buds receive radiant energy from the sun.

radiant energy. It's energy that is transferred by electromagnetic radiation such as light from the sun on to the peaches of the peach trees.

rootstock. It is the root portion of a grafted tree.

specie. Refers to the second part of a plant's botanical name. It's a group of organisms that can interbreed and produce fertile offspring comprising a species. These individual organisms can exchange genes.

spring equinox. Is the nickname for the "vernal equinox," which occurs on March 19 for year 2024 in the Northern Hemisphere. This is when the Earth's axis is tilted neither toward nor away from the sun, resulting in an equal amount of daylight and darkness at all latitudes.

stomata. Are a pair of guard cells on the leaf or stem of a plant that regulates carbon dioxide intake and releases oxygen into the atmosphere. Thus, it controls the water loss by changing the size of the stomatal pore.

transpiration. It is the loss of water vapor mainly through the stomata of plant leaves. Stomatal openings are necessary to absorb carbon dioxide into the leaf interior and by the same token to allow oxygen to escape into the atmosphere during photosynthesis.

tree crown. Refers to the total of an individual tree's above-ground parts, including stems, leaves, and reproductive structures.

variety peaches. There are three hundred varieties of peaches (*Prunus persica*) in the United States and over two thousand varieties globally. Some varieties of peaches are Earligrande type, Elberta type, Loring type, and Red Skins type.

wet spot spray. Refers to individual spraying of bacteria, fungi, bugs, insects, and weeds in spots of concern rather than spraying the entire field and/or peach trees. Some peach tree farmers claim that wet spraying is very effective spraying because the pesticide mixture is splashed on the spot that needs the solution, and since the mixture is wet, it stays on the spot longer; thus, it becomes more effective than regular spraying.

winter solstice. Solstice marks the onset of winter at the time of the shortest day of the year, occurs on December 21 for year 2023 in the northern hemisphere and June 21 in the southern hemisphere. As per the Old Farmers' Almanac, the winter solstice is the right time or shortly thereafter the best time to plant peach trees.

xylem. It's the vascular tissue in peach trees that conveys water and dissolved minerals upward from the root to the crown of the tree. It also helps to form the woody element in the stem of the tree to provide physical support.

ABOUT THE AUTHOR

Robert F. Rangel

Robert Rangel was born in Central Texas where the bluebell flowers grow wild and the Blue Bell ice cream is made. When Robert was a child, his father moved his family to the Texas Gulf Coast to work for Humble Oil Company where Robert grew up as a teenager. During his teen years, Robert's parents sent him to a farm in the summer to learn the art of farming. At the farm, Robert learned how to cultivate, plant, nurture, and harvest the food plants. Robert developed a passion for growing plants for human consumption. Since Robert spent three months out of the year at the farm, he was called the quarter farmer by some of the farmers.

After Robert graduated from high school, he enrolled in college to learn more about growing plants. Once he graduated from college, he taught biology and other science courses with emphasis in botany. After teaching for several years, Robert became a school principal. Although he no longer had direct contact with students, he encouraged teachers to teach science, emphasizing how to grow food plants.

When Robert retired from education, Robert wanted to continue his interest in growing food plants. It was during this time Robert discovered there was no one easy-to-reference source for people, such as him, to learn about growing peaches on a smaller scale designed for personal consumption. He began to perfect his peach planting techniques by planting two peach patches whereby he could experiment, conduct research, and explore a variety of techniques in order to achieve optimum results for growing peaches and writing a peach guide.

Today, Robert continues to farm by growing thousands of pine trees in Northeast Texas to produce lumber for America. Email Robert at peachguide333@aol.com for comments pertaining to the peach guide.